THEN AGAIN

First published in 2019 by
The Dedalus Press
13 Moyclare Road
Baldoyle
Dublin D13 K1C2
Ireland

www.**dedaluspress**.com

ISBN 9781910251430 paperback
ISBN 9781910251447 hardback

Dedalus Press titles are represented in the UK by
Inpress Books, www.inpressbooks.co.uk,
and in North America by Syracuse University Press, Inc.,
www.syracuseuniversitypress.syr.edu.

Cover image: *Female Figurines,* Leventis Municipal Museum
of Nicosia, Cyprus. Cover design: Pat Boran

The Dedalus Press receives financial assistance from
The Arts Council / An Chomhairle Ealaíon.

THEN AGAIN

PAT BORAN

DEDALUS PRESS

Contents

for Raffaela

Stillness

Like two startled meerkats
sensing a predator's approach –
the return of the king
from some battle, the arrival
of his wayward, 'inquisitive' son –
hoping not to be chosen
these two female servants
take a deep breath
then stand so utterly still
that not only the moment
but the greater part of recorded history
passes them by,
all the ugly intentions of the world
muttering to themselves as they vanish
back into the night.

Female Figurines, circa 1200 BC. Leventis Municipal Museum
of Nicosia, Cyprus

Race Meeting, Baldoyle

He smokes, she holds
something just below her nose, a sprig
of shamrock or wildflower snatched
from the roadside somewhere, something small
and fragrant that might lift the spirits
on this racecourse day – the bawl
of crowds, the thunder of hooves,
the scent of horseflesh and, out beyond,
the endless chugging of backed-up motorcars.
What holds the eye's and heart's attention
is the quiet that seems to link this pair
as words might do, the echoing postures,
his thick cigar, her petalled stem,
his solid, gruff uncertainty, her fragile,
dreamy elegance and grace. And, yes,
the one thing that the photograph commemorates
but has no chance of capturing: their breath.

Unidentified Miracles

for Janet McLean

Birds taking off
from a roadside bush –
contagion of ecstasy;

the dead man my father found
who, before the police turned up,
was back on his feet, ready
for another whiskey;

and this strange image,
three hundred years old,
of the day I was called by my father
to our long back yard
to witness his surprise, and spied,
in the low steel basin before him
filled to the brim, not
the thing he'd been studying
and wished now to reveal (a fish? an eel?
a hive of fresh-laid frogspawn?)
but a sky so empty and blue
that, before I knew it, it was,
in its own way too,
a kind of miracle.

*After a painting attributed to Pietro Novelli, Italian, 1603-1647.
National Gallery of Ireland*

Fountain

for Stuart Dischell

I loved it from the moment
I first saw it; turning the corner
in the midday sun – the soft
yellow limestone of Parisian façades
stretching off and away
to provide the perfect backdrop
of receding lines,
like a path in what might well have been
a woodland clearing a thousand years ago –
a green wrought iron drinking fountain
caught my eye, monument
to a gentle bubbling flame,
and on its polished rim
a small, dun-coloured bird
quietly taking its fill, obliging me
and all those there behind me
to stand and wait our turn
a few moments more
in the history of the civilised world.

Common Heron

for Mark Roper

Ruffled, dishevelled,
all claws and stilts,
a somewhat bewildered stare,
I'm grey-downed and -feathered,
a creature stepped out of a fog
wrapped in a cape;

entranced, intent,
reading the curving lines
in the wood of my case
like tracks in the sand,
rivulets caressing, inscribing
the estuary grains;

and darkness arriving
any time now, so they say,
but my bill's steely tip
is still steady,
still poised at the ink-well of night,
still ready to dip.

Natural History Museum, Dublin

The Big Freeze

After the closure of Emo Court as a Jesuit Seminary in 1969, statues of a number of classical female figures, (believed to have been consigned there by the former residents) were retrieved from the waters of Emo Lake

No one who has seen them will forget
the Jesuit novices out skating on the ice
of Emo Lake, that simple alphabet
of familiar poses – caution, doubt, surprise;

how they call to mind the Elder Bruegel's
sympathetic portraits of skating peasantry
in some tiny Flemish town, as the so-called Middle
Ages came to a close and this present

enlightened age of ours began.
And, of course, we have to love its innocence,
this dream-like masterpiece by Fr. Browne,
but my eye is drawn to something more intense,

more telling. It is winter 1938
and as Europe begins to brace itself for war
out on the ice ventures Leonard Shiel SJ,
unseen but by the unseen photographer.

And out there he demonstrates a bracket turn,
an arabesque, a perfect pirouette,
the bulk of his discarded great coat
ominous as a body by his feet.

Strange it could be so much colder then,
the trees not merely bare but skeletal,
the sky a bruise of greys, and the lake itself,
alien if at the same time magical,

scarred by the skater's blades as he goes,
unheeding of creaks, or groans, or the gentle rise
of pockets of trapped air from deep below –
the breath of the goddess marbling the ice.

Stalled Train

In the listening carriage, someone's phone
cries out for help. A student frisks himself,
a woman weighs her handbag
then stares into space. Our train
is going nowhere, stalled here
so long now the cattle in this field
have dared come right up close
to chew and gaze. We tell ourselves
that somewhere down the line
things we cannot understand
are surely taking place – the future
almost within reach – and into each
small telephone that rings
or shudders now, like doubt,
we commit (if still in whispers)
our hopes and fears,
our last known whereabouts.

The Art of Phrenology is Not Dead

When she sees him on *The News,* being led
down the courtyard steps to the waiting van,
my mother says: 'Oh, I don't like the look of him,'
meaning she wouldn't want to meet that face,
as his victim must have done, some dark night
when the rest of the population of the world
was around a corner, beyond a wall or hedge,
out of sight and reach. Of course, I laugh
sympathetically, reminding her that *The News*
has finished, that the killer with the 'dead eyes'
who troubles her so much is just an actor,
more likely than not a decent guy
from a good home, merely playing the part
he was chosen for, because of his looks.
My mother doesn't seem to hear. Perhaps
she thinks my protests are beside the point.
'Look at those eyes,' she goes on,
'the coldness in them, that hard jaw …'
And we debate and laugh, drink tea and chill
to the twists and ludicrous turns of the plot –
'I suppose we never know what people have
to cope with,' she admits after some time,
and we start into another pot of tea,
a middle-aged son and his 90-year-old mother
whose head, now I look closely, seems to shrink
between one visit and the next, whose mouth
is also smaller if no less soft, and whose own eyes,
though frightened lately, are as always searching
to find the good in everything they see.

Calligraphy

The last will and testament
of the Emperor Qin
instructs his eldest son
to take his own life.
Horrified and broken-hearted,
yet obedient to the end,
Fusu complies.

Fusu: the Heavens
stall in their turning,
the sea cannot move,
and out of the nightingale forest
no solace, no reprieve.

The world rumbles on.
Thus is the way made clear
for Huhai, Fusu's
keenest rival
and Qin's younger son –
he whose skills as a calligrapher
are second to none.

Robert

When I heard
he was dead
my once neigh-
bour and friend
Robert found
so they said
no, not drowned
as I'd guessed
(more than once
he had gone
to the shore
on his own
late at night)
but instead
in a press
a wardrobe
with his belt
round his neck
I was back
in my room
next to his
in that damp
grimy house
where we lived
long ago
would-be scribes
side by side
and he'd knock
rat-a-tat
now and then
on the pre-
text or need

of some milk
or a pen
to stand then
in the door
that warm smile
and a half
cigarette
on his lips
saying this –
did he say
it back then?
he for sure
says it now –
Thanks, I owe
you, we po-
ets must stand
each for each
must look out
for each ot-
her be twice
what we are
on our own
to be whole
in just words
and short lines
in small rooms
though no joke
all we have
to survive

The Wardrobe

for Fernando Trilli

At the foot of this enormous bed
the ancient wardrobe is a kind of church
or chapel, shrine to a local saint
whose relics were once kept safe within,
bestowing blessings
on these hillside woods, this house.

Now inside is emptiness itself, profound
absence, a gentle ache of pine;
yet every time I open and again
close tight its bright-grained door –
turning from the mirror of the self –
someone watches over me with kindness,
the empty hangers chime inside like bells.

The Bandleader

for Dick Sides

Call it strange or odd, but what we loved
when the marching band came proudly up the street,
the ranks of players following the heartbeat
of the big bass drum, was, up front, in white gloves,

tossing his baton above his head,
the bandleader, marking time. We stood and stared.
A lone guard, spectral at the crossroads,
directed traffic; children waved

to shy musician siblings, suddenly mature
in their outsized uniforms. But who could look away
from this feat of anti-gravity, his skillful, sure
mastery and control? Music played

and filled the valley of the street, echoing
off parked cars and plate-glass windows
where pale-faced dummies gazed like souls in limbo.
And yet, for all the toing and froing,

we loved it most when the band came to a halt
now and then, high stepping on the spot
but going nowhere, a panto horse
waiting for its rear end to catch up.

Odd to think that fifty years can pass
in the blink of an eye, that the world can change
so much and yet so little. But kids still like to march
and swing their arms. And if it seems strange

that a walking stick might suddenly transform
into a gleaming baton, who is he to complain?
He listens for the music he carries within him,
counts to himself, for a moment, then they're off again.

Lining Out

They were the big lads, the strong lads, the fit lads,
with their gum-shields and groin-guards, their county colour
    kit-bags;
we were the bozos in the hand-me-down sad rags,
alone in our windswept goalposts, looking on.

They were the boys with the thick-knit socks
and long-lace boots, calf muscles like rocks;
we were the castaways in castoff togs,
marooned in our windswept goalposts, just about clinging on.

They were the ones who made every squad,
up front in the bus, all fired up like Greek gods;
they were the named, the famed, the proclaimed and the cherished;

we were the slow ones, the 'Christ sake, would you go ons!',
the frozen half-dozen last to be chosen,
the nameless, shameless interchangeable no ones;
we were the AN Others at the end of the list.

Teenaged he-men descended from bears,
blood on their knees, mud in their hair,
they were the boys with the ice in their hearts and their veins;

we were the wasters, the dodgers, the slackers,
the double vest-wearers, the chocolate snack-packers,
the most likely to get the ball smack in the kisser and faint.

And then something happened, some fate struck a spark,
the wind changed direction, the bright sky went dark,
and the ball like a comet came down in our hands
and we held it –

And suddenly as one they rushed to our sides
in a flood of approval, a surge of pure pride,
to lift us up into the air on a tide of forgiveness;

and that sodden rectangle of tread-beaten grass
to the rear of the school – now the danger had passed –
was O'Moore Park or Croker itself and en masse
the 'they' and the 'we' were transformed, at long last, into 'us'.

The Way Things Are

Johnny cared. At a certain time of night
when we were drunk, and someone (often me)
was mouthing off about all the usual stuff –
how we would change the world, our generation,
how we had had enough of the hypocrisy
we saw around us everywhere – at that point
Johnny would finally wake up. 'Correct me
if I'm wrong,' he'd say, 'but is it good enough
that things are as they are, as if that were
reason enough for us to leave them be?'
And he'd start this rhetorical argument with himself
or whoever else was there, the waiter or waitress
when she came over to ask him, politely, to leave.
Then suddenly he'd be on his feet, fists
raised, voice bouncing off the four walls,
a kind of protection he'd throw around himself
when things got hot. 'You're asking me to leave?'
he'd roar. 'You're asking *me?*' And he'd look to us
for his defence. And we'd avoid his eyes
just long enough that he'd explode with anger.
And then, in seconds, he'd be dragged outside
while we stood, helpless, pleading with the bouncers,
to 'take it easy, he doesn't really mean it –
he's had too much to drink' – before, moments later,
we'd all be out, everyone together,
dazed and wasted and starting the recriminations
in the car park where he'd be shouting now at *us,*
his face ablaze, at *us,* with all his power,
blaming *us* for the state he'd gotten himself into
as we held him up and fumbled for the keys,
clambering into the car to sit there cursing
but unable to drive away because, of course,

whatever else he was when he was drunk –
slumped there on the tarmac in a puddle of spilled beer
and fresh piss so that we always had to wait
for him to burn the anger off and cool his heels,
the engine revving, the furry dice hopping
to the big beats on the deck – he was one of us.

Greek Vase

Play some romantic music
for these two brave fighters,
wrapped around each other here
like lovers, like old friends
reuniting, like drunks lunging
when the last bar closes
and they're tossed out into the night
throwing punches and poses
and holding each other tight –
for without each other, that's right,
they're all alone in the world.

Attic black figure lekythos, 550–510 BC, Paolo Orsi Museum, Siracusa, Sicily

Arena

The dozen or so young kids
playing football in the gravel and dust
of the Arènes de Lùtece
frankly couldn't care less
that gladiators once fought here,
were drawn off, dragging their heels,
or propped themselves up on a sword
while the mangled corpses of foes
were fed to wild beasts.
History is a long time ago.
Now only the spectators are real;
with each shot at their schoolbag goals,
watch as some 15,000 souls
rise howling to their feet.

Arènes de Lùtece, Roman Amphitheatre, Paris

After the Bonfire

So much for the wild abandon, the gangs
of teens and adolescents and admiring tots
building their teetering mountain of trash
defiantly all day long in the middle of the Green;
and forget the worried parents, even the ones
who, as the protest builds, themselves can feel
some old pull towards the heat, the chimney of yellow storm;
it's the kids who are back first thing the next morning
to the ashen wound in the grass, that last frayed string
of smoke from the carcass of shopping trolleys, bed springs
and broken glass, it's them I think of now,
that sister and brother, those lonesome waifs
who could not believe their luck last night
to be there at the centre of it all, and now,
in bright daylight, struggle to rekindle the flame.

A Lady Prepares a Meal

for Tulsi Badrinath

I feel I know her, the woman hunkered down
on this earthen floor, alone, preparing food,
among bowls and jars, an oblong grinding stone,
a folded towel, two fish just now unboned,
a sage or basil leaf, and the fire before her
breathing in her face. She seems to stare
into its depths, in wonder or devotion,
gazing through the moment of the task
into some greater narrative, the larger story
of our give-and-take existences. Ah meals,
what else is there to measure out our days?
So much goes on, off-stage, in rooms like these,
between the blast of saffron-coloured walls,
amid the smoke and slowly blooming steam,
in the years when we can manage still to squat
then stand again unaided to review
the mental list of things we've learned to do,
before the pinch – and just a pinch – of salt.

after a painting, c. 1810, Kangra, India. Chester Beatty Library, Dublin

The Pig's Eye

One is the handyman, struggling to unblock
the parish toilets for Confirmation Day.
'Father,' he tips his cap to the young priest
who's offered a bonus to have it fixed in time,
'For five bob, I'd drive shite to Heaven.'
Two is the 'poor unfortunate' who confided
to my mother that, after countless days
of bacon and cabbage, and yet more bacon and cabbage,
now and then she liked a change of menu –
cabbage and bacon. And number three is the neighbour
who joins my father's family now and then
for the feast that is the boiled head of a pig,
chanting, as my father loved to recall it,
'Give me the eye, for I love the eye.'
They are, of course, all of them, now gone,
half-blurred and anonymous, confused
one with the next in childhood's turf-smoke memory.
But what they have in common is forbearance
and grim humour. And, at a certain time of night
when yarns are told, they come to me again.
First is the man, clothes stinking to heaven,
limping home the road to a simple house
where a family group has gathered after labours,
the light of a lamp dancing on their one good blade.
A woman ladles cabbage water. Then someone
takes the blade and sinks it into the flesh
of a pig's head sat in the centre of the table,
while out of the darkness an aged neighbour asks
for the blessing of the eye. 'Give me the eye,'
all of them chime in, 'for I love the eye.'
And as an eye is duly ferried down
the length of that long table, each diner in turn,

grotesque now in the oil-lamp shadowplay,
grimaces and laughs, jeers and at last tucks in,
as if somehow they might sense us watching here
in a future of bewildering opportunity
and far worse kinds of poverty than their own.

The Catapult

To the rear of the house, a group of kids
has been out breaking glass with catapults
for the past half hour, remnants of a dozen bottles
scattered around the footpath when I arrive –
a base here, a partial neck stood there. I well recall
how good it felt, years back, to do
the very same myself, to set
a target down in place and pace
backwards slowly from it, measuring
with each step as I went, then reaching down
to choose from the entire planet Earth
the one stone truly equal to the task,
to set that one stone, carefully, neatly
into its cradle, draw back the elastic
until it creaked, all the while feeling
the growing tension in my arm,
my wrist, my pinching fingertips …
All day we shot, it might have been,
with cool and calm and clinical precision,
laying low the enemies we had conjured,
then imagining, as darkness fell and each of us
slipped away our separate ways, that we would
stand again as one when real enemies
came to seek us out in life.

And how simplistic that turned out to be.
Here, by your graveside, I'm back down on one knee.

Rue d'Ulm

for Clíona Ní Riordáin

There is always, when we look for it,
another life, a hint at least, a window
that overlooks the shaded courtyard,
a forbidding gate onto a bustling street
that opens to reveal a secret garden.
The woman in the small boulangerie
on my fifth visit finally ventures a smile
at my schoolboy French, and sets me wondering
if I might yet survive in attic exile,
in some mansard roof one-room
in a pile of papers, tossing in the night.
Stairways, balconies, all the stunning views
of spires and domes, the islands of green –
the other life is everywhere, a second tongue
waking up to tell the same truth differently.
In time, the novelty recedes
or fades; in time your eyes
look up less often, focussing straight ahead,
until one day, weighed down with shopping bags
from the local *supermarché*, who knows why,
but you take a different route, a parallel,
and find yourself emerging on a street
at the end of whose dramatically receding lines
the Panthéon is a spaceship silently hovering,
awaiting the order to carry you away.

After Rain

Last night, someone with a dog
came strolling down
this narrow cobbled street

about this hour,
a light fall of rain just passed
(as it has just now)

and, maybe pausing here,
admired, as I now do,
how light reflects

off the black volcanic stone,
the rippling sea of night
this golden city floats upon.

Last night, did I say?
I mean, of course,
two thousand years ago.

via Pompeo Picherali, Siracusa, Sicily

Sarcophagus of Giovanni Cardenas

Who could blame you, Giovanni Cardenas,
powerful citizen though you evidently were,
for choosing to face death with your faithful mongrel
crouching by your feet? What else is there

(impressive sword aside) that a soul could want
from this world of suffering but the unselfish love

of a creature who in darkness, as he did in light,
waits for you to wake and to set aside
like some old book what fears remain, then move
on through the long grass of the afterlife.

Sculpted by Antonello Gagini. 1506. Museo Bellomo. Siracusa, Sicily

Station Road, Sutton

There is that moment when the barrier comes down
on Station Road, when the train to Howth has passed
and nothing happens; when the men in lycra vests
and shorts on their blade-thin wheels look round

and through each other; when the yummy mums
with their dozy, school-bound offspring by their sides
or trussed up in the seats behind like dolls,
glance down one more time to check the time;

when the very birds up on that ever slack
tangle of cables shuffle two steps left
or one step right; when the sea retreats
and only sunlight advances along the track;

when something in the chest unlocks or shifts,
and you find you're no longer waiting; when the barrier lifts.

Rhododendron Gardens, Howth

Some days when I walk this hill,
following my dog up the first steep steps
Through ferns and nettles, then on and up
into the ever-thickening rhododendron woods,
their unreal, hallucinogenic blooms
like Chinese lanterns, I imagine there,
on the opposite side, and climbing too
at a more-or-less similar, steady pace,
another man with another dog,
advancing with the same determined strides
I fall into unthinkingly –
until, emerging from thick leaf-shade
into open air, we crest the peak
together, two dogs, two men,
each pair circling the other
before moving off on the trace of a scent
or the glimpse of something far off
across parks, and roads, and housing estates,
the sun reflecting in a single windowpane.

The Steps

How long have they been here,
these half a dozen small steps coarsely hewn
into the limestone breakwater down
at the local bathing spot, for months now
eclipsed by the new disco bar, an alien craft
on stilts, descended from the sky
at the start of summer

until last week's unexpected storm
pummelled, pounded and stripped it right back
to this rusted, rattling skeleton of itself
ringed by floating debris, and the steps
stood clear again, still doing nothing
but leading down into the gently lapping sea,
and yet, in this cold-morning, post-storm light,
so old it seems they might be rising up.

Belvedere San Giacomo, Siracusa, Sicily

Plate

If you look closely, holding your breath,
you can almost see him step
from one green leaf to the next,
the bird on this hand-painted plate
you're unable to pass. The gold
and blue of his plumage
echoes the motion blur
that decorates the outer ring,
as if, plucked out of time,
this is but a single still
from the short film of a life
before film exists. The plate
as globe and cosmic wheel. The plate
as article of faith: *Please God,*
we will eat today, the sun
will fall then rise and, if we are blessed,
that bird we glimpsed just yesterday
will come again to sit
and sing in our tree, the world
turned upside-down in its ecstasy:
the blue of the sea in its feathers,
the tamed sun
perched on its dazzling breast.

Decorated plate. 1788 AD. Leventis Municipal Museum of Nicosia, Cyprus

Pocket Watch

In my own museum
of things I can't let go of (or
that won't let go of me) –
among the boxed-up memories,
the pterodactyl-black umbrellas,
and my first old typewriter, still
like some crouching gargoyle
readying to pounce – there is
my father's pocket watch. The chain
is long since broken, the glass face
scarred by one and then another
of the hundred million seconds
it tried its best to measure
as they tumbled past. But what I love now
is its emptiness, its resistance,
that insistence on being right
once a day and again each night –
that and the effort required
not only to turn but even just
to pinch and hold that tiny
winding mechanism it extends
pointlessly in space. Like falling
towards the mystery of a black hole,
it slows me down, calms
some hurt I don't have time
to dwell on any more.
Forget the date, the when and why.
What I admire, if not too much,
are the hands spread open there
at 8 and 2, as if to say: *Me?*
I've nothing to hide, I've no regrets.

The best we can hope for from this life
is to be left like this, empty-handed,
like the fisherman recalling
the one that got away.

Pocket Watch. 20th century. Leventis Municipal Museum of Nicosia, Cyprus

Bus Stop

James Fintan Lalor Avenue, Portlaoise

The world is full of beautiful places;
this isn't one of them. Decades back
a line of trees stood here, a gate,
and open fields I half-remember
from a morning walk, the world spread out
and, in that early light, all glistening.

But time moves on, the land
bends to our will. Where cattle dreamt,
now townsfolk come to meet, to shop,
and, like me here, to stop and wait
inside this wind-swept, glass-walled hut
for the wheels of change
to carry them away. We would be
anywhere some days
but where we are.
                              And yet last week,
as I sat here on this backside-numbing bench
a man right here beside me took a call.
'Sheila?' His voice was quivering.
'What's that? You're in the clear?
Oh Sacred Heart of Christ,' he said, 'Thank God!'
And, before I might do anything, he'd reached
across and hugged me, held me, his ageing fingers
trembling now like grass, his face against mine
damp – and I can feel it still – as early mist.

Roundabout

Roundabout. You could call it that.
You could find a quiet dark space
inside yourself and name it,
why not, Roundabout. As good
as anything. Hollow, Longing,
Artichoke, Rose …

Breaking the mystery down
into the vaguely known, the familiar
constituent parts. Like those names
that evoke the many hidden forces –
Sirocco, Libeccio, Tramontane –
when all it is is wind. When all you mean
is what's just up ahead, the unnameable thing.

Prayer for a Grieving Sister

Your death's undone her,
as if she were a thing
of air and luck … And now
she can't let go, your sister,
or step away. She can't move on.
And these spring nights, like all
the winter nights before them,
you hear her turn the key and, slow
as a funeral procession, wander off
she knows not where, soft
or hard rain falling on her skin,
her shadow lengthening
then vanishing
as darkness takes her
back to sit in silence
by your grave, the grave
the cruel gods have dug
just yards from home …

Two years you are gone already,
and, free of all we cling to here –
these lengthening evenings, laughter, drink,
the dance of music on the breeze –
if you can bear to sense or feel
something of her pain, reach down,
lost brother, touch her face,
send a sign she'll know has come
from you alone, a tune
in the air, your whistling signature,
then take her hand and hold it
and, as only you can do, lead her
out of this dark shadow world

that she might live again, her breath
her own, her heart set free once more,
her rigor mortis grip on grief released.

Hitchhiker

All I did was drive.
No promise of a bargain up ahead,
hard or soft, the coastal skies
full of colour borrowed

from the slowly lowering disc of sun
and the dust of a volcanic interruption
that all that week had caused a run
on ferry tickets, commotion

in the airports and, for one good friend,
left him stuck in France
with a girl, like himself, at a dead end
and thinking, well if this is it, let's dance.

The radio was playing so I didn't really care
that he said nothing, the music minor, slow,
and when we reach our destination and the stranger
gathered his things to go,

it seemed he might be from another time
and visiting ours, the way he took my hand
to signal his appreciation, his smile
a mere flicker in the air, if that,

halfway between glimpse and apparition,
meaning without the need for words,
his wave in the rear-view mirror
a flare, a flurry, a flight of birds.

Strokkur Geyser

for Hrafn Andrés Harðarson

For a decade now
off and on
I've been thinking
how there had to be
a poem there
when we stood on the ice
by the Strokkur Geyser
and Hrafn conjured
a boiling cauldron
the size of a football stadium
under our feet.
How could anyone
fail to find
the poetry in such a moment?
And yet I did,
over and over.
And now this morning
those ten years
have become their own
vast and mysterious space,
and here I am again
seeing only
the thin jet of pressure,
the after-effect,
the evaporating steam.

Estuary

'Soon there will be no birds left at all,'
says the elderly man on the bench
overlooking the estuary where a dozen curlews
bend to stitch the frayed edge of blue silk.
It has been so calm, so still all day.
Maybe he is my myth visitor,
come to impart some unwanted darker news.
I sit beside him. Whatever he has read
is already haunting him, the ink
on his fingertips. We talk for hours,
until, silver-grey, the evening tide slips in
around our feet. Tonight I dream
of the last curlew flying across the estuary,
of ink stains unfolding slowly through the water.
I wake to inspect the landscape of my hands,
seeing them, as might a seabird or a drone,
so powerless, so small, so far away.

Virgin of the Crossroads

for Pilar Villar Argaiz

Not long ago there were,
on country crossroads like these,
statues of the Virgin. A little shrine
of rocks and flowers, herself
in pink and blue and white,
maybe a votive candle or two
pooling at her feet. My father
would slow a little as we passed,
then, abruptly blessing himself,
announce it was time to proclaim
one or other variant of the mystery,
and we'd sigh or groan,
knowing it was futile to resist.
Before we'd finished
the extended litany
of the Hail Holy Queen, his mood
would brighten now he'd done
his bit to keep a godless future
at arm's length. And he's with me
still tonight, you know,
driving late on this winding
country road, heading homewards,
rounding a bend to find her
stood there still
in this winter's night, a solitary girl
waiting for her bus,
her face beatific
in the light of her mobile phone.

51

Bus Journey

The faces in the windows to either side look back,
rain-streaked and pale, surprised we could believe
we are going in the same direction, as if
it should be obvious by now that all these journeys
on which we set out feeling oddly unified,
at one with each other, before the depot fades
and shrinks to insignificance again,
lead to moments of division and sub-division;
the trance takes over; the back and forth
and back again of all such trips
begins to take its toll. We journey out
through nothingness, the distant glow
of something like a memory unbound. Bright lights
flash past on poles, like stylite saints
whose names we can't recall. And when at last
we reach the end of the road, shades of our selves,
shed layers of skin, we leave our ghostly images
on board, withdrawing from them, stepping down
to dumb reality again, to draw our luggage
from the rumbling hold and, ballasted once more
by the actual, glance up at the departing glass
where there is nothing now but city lights,
a great absence passing through itself.

The Door Bell

The previous house we lived in –
battered, broken, neglected
by the side of the road –

is offices now, everything
but the brickwork replaced
and the Georgian door,

the bell no longer connected
to anything, and cold
from the constant touch of passing ghosts.

The Children of Alcoholics

The children of alcoholics
make fine actors,
in broken homes, hurting homes,
learning from an early age
to deceive, to deflect
attention, when all else fails
to put a brave face on.

Look now, here they come,
the bright, the bold, the beautiful.
They kiss the air when they meet,
they stand upright and proud,
in darkness, speaking calmly,
confidently to the gods,
then bow and close their eyes
to vanish, if only for a moment,
in the wave-wash of applause.

And they need our love so much,
these hurting creatures,
that, somehow, sensing it,
we laugh and cry along with them,
freeing smaller hurts inside ourselves,
our applause and our tears –
if only they could be bottled –
as precious, as potent,
as addictive as alcohol.

Desire

Lift the roofs off this row of houses
and who might we prove to be:
kids playing video games in flickering light,
an old man reading the newspaper, stopping
to double-check the date; a girl on the floor
of her room, twisting and stretching herself
to undo some vague pain; and a young man
alone, wearing headphones, tending
the lonely flame of desire.

But zoom in now a little closer
and that could be you and me down there,
waltzing around our steam-filled kitchen
as if on the deck of an ocean liner
inching outwards through the thickening fog.

Gaza, North Dublin

After hours of play
our two adolescent sons
stretch out in this small back garden,
close their eyes and dream.
For a moment they might be
the beautiful Palestinian children
from last week's news,
the same dark skin, the dark hair
haloed by flowers,
nothing at all to suggest
what befell them
or what is yet to come –
only their clothes rearranged
in haste to conceal
the bruises that, on this earth, are
the only maps
that cannot be redrawn.

Skateboarders

Wearing our new wide-angle action cams
we roll into town; the bus ride, the vault
over ticket stiles and spooling escalators,
exposing the balding skulls and down-blouse jewels
of fellow travellers. And out into the city's open arms.

All day we're on the streets, outside the bank
with the concrete seats that double up as rails
and lips. We jump, we leap
to keep the heart beats beating, to free
ourselves from you and your enslavement
to the gravity of the past. What else is there?
Come on, you need to ask?
The flight. Reflected light. The void
you ride when you rise beyond the ramp.

The Medal

i.m. Michael Delaney

My grandfather came home from war
shell-shocked, 'raving in the night',
my mother said, the clothes kicked off his bed
as if the blankets were of mustard gas or the mud
that continued falling when the shelling stopped.

I never knew him, but I sensed an open wound
whenever he was mentioned in dispatches.
As we grew older we tried new ways to ask
about what happened out there in some field.
That small medal served him like a shield.

In the National Museum of Ireland

We have spent too long in the dark
and they are tired and growing irritable
when the older spots a cabinet
of medieval swords – the sheer sharp reach
of the hand-made blades, four feet long at least
from hilt to tip, impossible to resist;
and suddenly they are spirited away.
I might risk something bright or funny –
as fathers will at times like this –
but, when I turn to look, the older,
with an arm around his brother's shoulder,
leads the other slowly towards the door
through gleaming silence, the pair of them
just about staggering clear of something glimpsed
and chilling, boy soldiers both,
leaving, for now, the battlefield behind.

Yataghan

It might be bone or rhino horn or ivory,
the handle of this 19ᵗʰ-century sword
from the Ottoman world, designed for close-up fighting,
the enemy's breathing inseparable from your own.

Perhaps that's why, after all these years,
the three bright jewels embedded in the hilt
conjure not so much the spoils of war, the thrill,
as a drop of blood, a bead of sweat, a single tear.

Turkish short sabre. Leventis Municipal Museum of Nicosia, Cyprus

Falling

Something in me loves when someone falls
in slow-motion – the accident, the grief
somehow given grace and meaning –
that awkward turn, that twist, the perilous leaning
followed by that face-front fall into disgrace
becomes a kind of ballet of intent, the body
struggling to honour gravity and space,
going all out, giving of itself in an act
of self-abandonment, at swim
in emptiness, drowning in nothingness,
and, even still, raising its arms in praise.

Saxophone Music

for Sinéad MacAodha

Someone's playing saxophone
in the topmost window of a building
on a Paris street,
across the way
from where I'm standing
stripped to the waist,
waiting for the technician to leave the room
and the giant cold screen
I'm pressed up close against
to take its precious X-Ray
of my lung.
           The sound is long and breathy;
deeply I inhale.
           I'm not as young
as I think I am, and might never
pass this way again. So, later,
as I dress, already I am
imagining my return, determined
to make this dreaming last all day –
a sojourn in the library
that is the Luxembourg Gardens,
(with a pause to tip the busker on the gate),
then the shortcut up rue Pierre et Marie Curie,
and home again to rue des Irlandais.

Lung Collapse

It was like the night the marquee tent,
in a gale that came in off the sea,
twisted so violently this way and that
that it crumpled into itself with a wheeze

and ended up flat, flat as the shape
the TV detective traces with chalk
round a corpse, until wear and tear
wash it away. But if that's what it was,

his 'lung collapse' – or whatever they said,
the older kids – I lay there all night
unable to sleep, in my mind's eye
the elephants, clowns and acrobats

left there with nothing over their heads
but empty sky, endless dark,
and, in the back field, chugging away,
the petrol generator of his heart.

Compost

i.m. Danny Rogers

After his wife died, then his Spanish lover, after he himself almost died, and not just once, went wild with grief and just about came back to settle on the bright side of the thin divide between nothingness and here, my old friend fell in love – he swore he fell in love – with compost.

Compost, compost; compost and little else he talked about for days on end when we spent too much time sat in the pub where he put Schopenhauer and Freud and even Little Richard temporarily aside in order to enthuse and, like some aged Christ standing in the marketplace, regale the local dropouts and assorted student types with tales of rot and regeneration, going on and on, but never boring, though close as a soul might come, on the subject of compost.

The death and the remaking of the world. The slow transformation that prompted him to slow himself down and learn at last to see. That's what he saw and wanted each of us to recognise. The worms and beetles working in the shade, in the shadow, in the theatre of darkness in which we alone get to prance about on stage. The little threads the fungus weaves, the life come snaking out from one short helix of potato peel or one sweet apple core. The thickening, greening, browning, blackening into slime of, really, everything, lifeless heaviness turning to that stunning powder that is the lightest talc on earth, carrier of zest and zip, vigour and vim. Compost, and compost yet again. The one fit subject.

One night he woke me, from his sleeping bag on the living room floor, still half asleep after a day of tunes and booze, and going on as ever about compost. It's the food of the gods, he croaked, and I said, Would you for Christ's sake go to sleep? and shut the door. And I half expected him to start to make some there, in my chill flat at the heart of the city, sixty-odd miles from the heap he could scarcely bear those days to be separated from. The navel of the world, the omphalos, as the Greeks called it, in his small back yard.

Two decades on, when we lost him too, a lonely frightened joker-king as the curtain fell, did I not almost immediately think of all his rambling, hilarious, obsessive talk of compost? And grim vision though it is, of my friend himself as compost? To be sure I did. The dark ferment and fermentation. The break-up, breaking down, the shifting round of what this life starts out with and never ceases to renew or reinvent. The seed, the pith, the spore ... Night after night I awoke, as once he did, with compost in my head.

And then, slowly, the gradual return, the change, the lift, the puff of smoke, that inching back and up, at last, like memory, out of the dark, up through the layered silence, the first words pushing clear - my old friend fell in love - like the slow-emerging tendrils of new growth, tenuous and strange, up through the rich, thick canvas that is compost for the first time then, and then again, then little by little, day by day by day.

Force 10 in Belmullet

i.m. Dermot Healy

In Belmullet, in the back room
of a bar, playing pool with Dermot Healy
while the grey Atlantic batters the lean-to roof,
he and I alternate between pints and shorts,
shorts and pints, stopping for a bit
for a toasted ham-and-cheese as he begins
to chalk up his cue with a faraway look then generously
leans across and begins to chalk up mine –
for the longest time, as if his mind
is elsewhere, composing something, sensing
something about to manifest in the air,
allowing me to return the favour
by buttering his toast, buttering
so slowly, so carefully, outwards from the centre,
that, for a moment, we see ourselves
as if from elsewhere, a pair of strangers
in the silver coastal light
of our brotherhood, hungover
but unexpectedly fulfilled, the novice
smoothing the vellum, the reluctant master
tending to the quills.

Expulsion from the Garden of Eden

If no one told you this was Adam and Eve
being driven out of Eden, you might imagine
two much more recent refugees –
the same heartache, the same stunned disbelief –
but we are standing in a holy place
and see only what we've learned to see.

Masaccio. Santa Maria del Carmine, Florence

Graveyard Scene

The morning so cold,
the earth so utterly iced over,
a child asks her mother
how the gravediggers will dig out a hole
for her friend. The mother
smiles, around them
other adults lost in veils
of breath, the vapour-clouds
of self, reminders of how
insubstantial all of this is:
the gates, the headstones,
the path through the forest of dates
on their way to this place
where the priest lifts his hands
to intone, watched over
by patient, shivering children
and buxom angels
in their lingerie of stone.

A Dying Craft

The little shop was one of those
that sells new things made to look old:
mildewed mirrors flecked with dust,
metal picture-frames whose rust

has carefully been faked with paint –
perhaps by children far away
in rooms where dust and rust and mould
are worth, it would appear, their weight in gold.

Saturday Morning in Magione

i.m. Macdara Woods

Saturday morning, an engine turning over
in the distance; outside the small café,
vespas on the footpath, local traders,
grumbling about tax, stirring espressos,
smoking from one pack; and across the street
a clutch of teens goes drifting in to school,
fog still stretched along the valley floor,
the sheets the world is reluctant to throw off.

Late Delivery

for Jimmy Murphy

When your father died
we drove by the house
one last time,

you in the family car,
me on a sputtering Honda 70,
death's outrider.

A minute passed,
the windows of the cars reflecting
roof tiles, chimney stacks ...

And then, as we pulled out
in a staggered train, a postman
approached the empty house.

Junk mail, postcards, bills?
Who's to say. But it stayed with me,
the odd timing of it –

an oddness that repeats:
I was 50 miles away,
reading a poem by Keats

for a CD recording –
the sedge has withered from the lake,
and no birds sing –

when I got the news
of my own father's death. In shock
I sat and read it through ...

as if words arrive
too late anyway, the notes we drop
through a chink of light.

Event Horizon

Lee, aged 4

As black holes
have invisible boundaries
that cannot be crossed,

we can only dream
of a starting point
to time and space,

across a line
which our finest minds
at best approximate.

Tell that to our son,
cracking the fridge door open
again and again,

determined to see
what, if anything, exists
before the light comes on.

The Old Year

i.m. Dennis O'Driscoll

The old year has nothing left to lose.
The shelves are cleared, the last of the bread is gone,
and, in the blue-white, ice-cold light, just two
unfortunate school-leavers carry on

in slow motion, setting out in place
tomorrow's miracles — fruit from far-off lands,
vacuum-packed or freeze-dried, seeds and grains
harvested in the great outdoors to stand

like patients in their paper uniforms – and doubt
still nagging us as we go strolling by,
our trolleys like so many gaping mouths
to be refilled. Tonight

your absence is everywhere, in the chill
breath of fridges, in these half-price treats
and Best Before tags. I pause to read
a frozen ready-meal and feel

and faraway as anyone can be
and still be living. And if I push on
with all these luxuries and few necessities,
it is to hear the till's electric song

and picture you, some long-gone Saturday,
the deal done, order once more restored,
your list of items ticked off and filed away,
kids sweeping up, the future at the door.

20th Anniversary

08.02.2019

From his new doorway of earth
my father looks up to admire
the star-filled sky,

just as, on Main Street, for years
he would pause, fixing his collar,
watching the world go by.

Cenicero (La Rioja, Spain)

for Melania Terrazas Gallego

In Cenicero's only bar & restaurant
the card players are mostly older men
who've reached retirement age, and now, most days,
pass an hour or two in the small front bar
scowling, looking tough, or sat on chairs
out front to smoke before the weather turns,
while those like us who come from far beyond
the limits of their no-frills hilltop town
the Romans called 'the ashtray' settle down
in the larger, almost hidden room behind
to discuss the menu of the day: jambon,
eels, chard, all the flora and fauna
these hardy locals have shared this landscape with
since the first mist cleared these stubborn hills
like a lingering doubt, since the first red wine
made here countless centuries ago
was tasted, frowned at and, approvingly, spat out.

Le Vernissage

for Stéphane Gherbil

Just before the preview of the show,
le vernissage – the varnishing or glazing –
the stage manager, with all the lights and screens
at last in place can get back to the basics,
turning his attention to the things
that matter most, the floor, the doors, the walls,
the eleventh-hour erasing of the scrapes
and scuffs, all the unintended interactions
of everyone who has lately passed this way,
himself included in all the full-on and four-square
non-stop preparations of these past few days –
until it comes to this: a room well-lit
and open-mouthed in anticipation,
all that any artist needs, and more,
the fabled welcome, the waiting neutral space.

Astronaut

On his way to the moon, the astronaut
meets his mother – the openness
of her face, her black hair
flecked with starlight. She kisses him,
whispers his name, her breath
gentling on his skin. He feels
tears rise within him, his heart
beats so hard he thinks
surely he will die up here,
so far from home … But his mother
consoles him, strokes his cheek,
calms his frantic thoughts,
holds him steady
in her steady, kindly gaze.
Thank you, he says
in a whisper, floating
at the edge of sleep.
She promises to stay –
if he would like her to –
a little longer,
and to leave on, for a while yet,
the small blue light of Earth.

Homeless Man and Dog

Look at them kiss, the homeless man and his dog.
Never underestimate the love
of pets. The dog doesn't know it's homeless,
and the man, for a moment, forgets.

Ha'penny Bridge

Collecting coppers on an Irish flag –
a spectre in a Simpsons sleeping bag.

The Spire (10 years on)

The spire in the quagmire,
The dagger in the corpse,
The skewer in the sewer,
The middle finger up.

The stiffy by the Liffey,
The ace in the hole,
The chopstick stuck in traffic,
The North(side) Pole.

The pin that burst the bubble,
The last tooth in the comb,
The first sign of trouble,
The barbed welcome home.

The spike in the crime rate,
The spine without a back.
The hypo from the Corpo,
The stake through the heart.

The needle in the noodle,
The point of no return,
The stick in the muddle,
The javelin, the harpoon.

The rod, the birch, the bata,
The Christian Brother's cane,
The crozier of St. Patrick
Weaponized again.

The flagpole flying nothing,
The blade-like glint of steel,
The arrow pointing nowhere,
The raver's broken heel.

Stiletto in the ghetto,
Monument of blight,
The nail in the coffin,
The 'we' reduced to 'I'.

The Password

Locked out, yet again, and running out of patience,
despite all the bright inventions that cannot fail –
the online wallets, the nagging one-word prompts,
the ghost in your mind of a page behind the page –
we're left to misremember and second-guess:
your name, my name backwards, Password itself?
Nothing works. It seems the dog can sense
the rising tension and slinks away to stretch
his long form out behind the white net curtain,
a spy in our midst, concealed behind a veil.
Your date of birth, my first car's registration …
All day we've tried and tried then walked away,
muttering, grumbling, to our parental duties,
to come back later, humbled, to the very same
bloody impasse – Please enter your password,
observed now by the very moon and stars,
until, somehow, with the cuff of my shirt sleeve
I manage accidentally to touch Return
and, simple as that, it opens, and we're in,
reminded that long before we became so stuck
and clueless here, so stressed by the simple things,
there was, remember, nothing whatsoever between us.

Learning to Moonwalk

Sometimes it's worth doing things
the wrong way around, stopping half-way
then moving backwards towards the starting line.

Like the day I broke your vase
by accident and, even as it fell, felt something
close to horror (wisdom, some would say) –

once it was clear I'd lost it anyway –
tugging me back, holding me there,
long enough to watch it fall, to see it strike

and splash across the bright-tiled floor
in so hypnotic an undoing
that, even as the moment found itself

in awed completion, already it was plain
that I might watch it fall again and still again
yet fail to grasp that, every blessed time,

like hope, like love itself, the ropes
unravelling over years or, all of a sudden,
split in two and whipping past our eyes,

this frozen sea of glass could not be kept
intact, was doomed to shatter like a wave
about my feet, less error than some simple twist

of fate conferring on this one unworthy man
the gift of hindsight. So see me, world,
the lonely fool who knows it's past

too late, that things have gone beyond
the point of all return, my eyes half-shut,
my mind closed to the flags and facts,

moonwalking here across the kitchen floor,
the water in the taps full on
my stadium audience calling out for more.

Making the Bed

Alone, the job is pretty much impossible,
each breeze amplified, the merest flick
enough to spill the whole lot on the floor
like a roof of snow. And yet the effort
conjures better days when you and I
would make the bed together, once more
stretching a sheet out crisp and taut and flat,
then slowly lowering to watch it swell and sigh
and, at long last, to settle after all,
the flag of the republic of our love
that afterwards might break our loving's fall.

Dysart Woods (Stradbally, Co. Laois)

from dísert, *a hermitage; prob.* out of Latin deserta, *a desert or lonely spot*

Midlands-bound to see my mother
wrapped in blankets in her nursing home
(despite the upturn in the weather),

I break the journey at Dysart Woods
to run the dog and clear my head
in the landscape of childhood.

Along the curving path, one tree
stands out among all the rest
that echo it. A common beech,

it branches, at about face-height,
into two, then, higher up,
a few feet closer to the light

(a year or two, perhaps, in time)
seeming almost to doubt themselves
the two parts merge back into one

before, farther up again,
the one divides, and spreads, and spreads,
that indecision left behind …

The dog, nose down, tail in the air,
freed from his captivity,
dashes ecstatically here and there,

with leaves to dig, phantoms to chase;
while I just stand here, lost in thought
in this lonely, oddly holy place

of trees and trees and still more trees,
the keening, ancient wind, this heart
torn open by its urgent need to heal.

This is a Book

i.m. Philip Casey

This is a book. It is what happens
when the batteries die, when the lights
go out, when the wires that join the world
into the fantasy of connectedness
run cold. Somewhere, somewhen,
a man sat down, a woman cleared
a space in the riot of a sunlit room
or lamplit cave, a hospital bed
or the rocking bunk of a boat far out
at sea – and began to dream.
This book, and the words it was made
to protect, came later, and was far
from guaranteed. And even now, who knows –
and this is the dream of every book –
a talking dog or walking table,
a land of such great beauty the gods
require two suns to do it justice,
comes to life, and lives each time
these words made of ink like tiny plants
respond to the light, a passing breeze
or a breath turns over the page.

The Beaten Track

As if some part of you still half-expects
to return some day and, somehow, walk again
the same streets of the same forgotten cities,
your wallet, bags and suitcases still cling
to the small change of a dozen foreign lands.
And every now and then you weigh a coin,
trying to conjure the image of a place,
a face, the exotic music of a name,
and find there's nothing left. Yet here and there,
at angles to the world, the real and dreamt
meet at little corner shops and bars
where the friendly waitress offers a free top-up
while the barman continues to shine the countertop
which starts out vague as any blemished wood
but, before you leave, has come up clear as glass.

ACKNOWLEDGEMENTS

Acknowledgements and thanks are due to the following where a number of these poems, or versions of them, were previously published or broadcast:

The Irish Times, The Examiner, Cadences (Cyprus), *Poetry Café* (Korea), *North* (UK), *Live Encounters, Arena* (RTÉ Radio 1), *Poetry Ireland Review* and *The Poetry Programme* (RTÉ Radio 1), and to the following anthologies: *Everything to Play For: 99 Poems About Sport,* ed. John McAuliffe (Poetry Ireland, 2015); *The Lea-Green Down: poets inspired by the poetry of Patrick Kavanagh,* ed. Eileen Casey (Fiery Arrow Press, 2018) and *The Strokestown Anthology 2017 & 2018*. 'Gaza, North Dublin' was published in *Sendiana,* a Solidarity Broadsheet for Palestine, edited by Catherine Ann Cullen, 2018.

'Bus Stop' was commissioned for the Laureate na nÓg anthology *Once Upon a Time,* compiled by Eoin Colfer (Little Island Books, 2015). 'The Big Freeze' for written for a poetry and music event in July 2018 at Emo House, Co. Laois.

'Lining Out' was first broadcast on *Sunday Miscellany,* RTÉ Radio 1. A film version was produced by RTÉ Sport and broadcast on TV to mark the 2017 All-Ireland Senior Football Final. The online version was viewed and shared more than 300,000 times that week.

'Station Road, Sutton' and 'The Spire (Ten Years On)' were both included in *If Ever You Go: A Map of Dublin in Poetry and Song,* eds. Gerard Smyth & Pat Boran (Dedalus Press, 2014), as was 'Ha'penny Bridge', the latter also being included in the anthology of the same name, edited by Mike English and published by Dublin City Council. 'The Spire' was issued as a handpress limited edition poster by Jamie Murphy of the Salvage Press in 2014. The poem featured in the anthology *Windharp:*

Poems of Ireland Since 1916, edited by Niall MacMonagle (Penguin Ireland, 2015). It was also set to music by Roger Gregg of Crazy Dog Audio Theatre and, in September 2015, a choral setting by Stephen Gardner was performed by New Dublin Voices in Dublin's GPO and Dubin City Gallery, The Hugh Lane.

The author is grateful to the following for periods of residency, festival invitations and other forms of support which resulted in poems in this book being written: Sophie Kandaouroff and all at the Château de Lavigny, Vaud, Switzerland; Sinéad MacAodha and the staff of the Centre Culturel Irlandais, Paris; Fernando Trilli and all at Immagini d'Irlanda, Umbria, Italy; Sven Kretzschmar, Pilar Villar Argaiz and Melania Terrazas Gallego of the EFACIS Irish Itinerary, Spain, 2018; and Nora Hadjisotiriou and Lily Michaelides of the 3rd International Literary Festival, Nicosia, Cyprus, in 2017, and all at the Leventis Municipal Museum of Nicosia.

Many thanks to Theo Dorgan for his friendship, his encouragement and his always keen eye.

Finally, a number of these poems were written or revised on a solo visit to my Sicilian in-laws in October 2018; to them, as ever, my warm and sincere thanks for the home away from home.

Lightning Source UK Ltd.
Milton Keynes UK
UKHW040712220219
337793UK00003B/5/P